Standards

A Guide to High School Coxing

By

Loryn Schopke

Loryn Schopke

ISBN 9781496007391

LCCN

Printed in the United States of America

Acknowledgments

I would like to thank my consultant, Mr. Nelson, for helping me work through the publishing and editing process. I would not have been able to publish this book without his help.

I would like to also thank my coach, Ethan Shoemaker, for both assisting me in writing my book as well as guiding me in my career here on Space Coast.

I would like to thank the men's team of Space Coast Crew for providing me with the experience and support for the material of this book.

I would also like to thank Daniel Vital, an alumnus coxswain of Space Coast Crew, who continued his coxing career into college and gave his own insight from a college coxswain's perspective.

I would also like to thank my family for supporting me and providing me with what I needed to accomplish writing this book.

Loryn Schopke

I would like to dedicate this book to my team, Space Coast Crew. You guys mean the world to me and I expect great things in the future both near and far as we take on the next steps in making a name for ourselves.

Table of Contents

Preface

What I really want you to understand first, is that every team is different and works differently. I know that you picked this up thinking, "thank the lord there is a book on how to do this right," but that is not what this is. This isn't a rule book. These are suggestions from myself and others based on what we have seen and what we have done. Let it be known that this is written from the perspective of a high school coxswain of a club team; making any of this information subject to question and it may not even be right at all, but even if it is wrong it is not due to a lack of understanding of what you're faced with. You try tirelessly, arrive early, leave late, listen to your rowers, listen to your coach, organize, set up, put away, and take responsibility. It is a seemingly thankless position; you will be criticized heavily for one mistake while several accomplishments get no praise at all, and you will love every second of it. The problem I have with our role and the one I hope to address with this guide, is that the standard for what we do is perfection, yet we are expected to teach ourselves most of what it takes to actually be a coxswain. It is a seemingly impossible task, and even with this guide you will beat yourself up for the simplest of mistakes. However, it is at the utmost importance for you to realize and accept that, contrary to popular belief, it is ok to make mistakes and to be wrong, because you will be. You have the most difficult job on the water (I can safely say that because I was a rower once, but I still wouldn't go around telling that to your rowers) and it is impossible for you to always make the right decision. So this book is to assist in developing your confidence as a coxswain and as a leader, because that is what we are.

"As a coxswain, I concentrated most on knowing the people in my boat - why they were rowing, why they came down to the boathouse, what made them tick. You have to know whether someone's rowing because they love their mother and hate their father. They're not sure they are proud of themselves; they want to be proud. Determine some of that and you can tap the strongest parts of those individuals. Being able to inspire someone, unexpected and in a way new and fresh to them, is what made coxswaining special for me." -- Devin Mahoney, Coxswain, Varsity Heavyweight Eight, Harvard '86

Standards

"An indecisive cox, like an ambivalent surgeon, is worse than useless. Wherever he goes, with whatever he says or touches, he sows confusion and disorder. The coxswain must seize control, take command of the boat and crew long before the shell ever leaves the dock." - (Mind Over Water)

"Decisiveness is even more important on the water, where many more unruly factors come into play. The greater the degree of surrounding chaos, the more crucial it becomes to have confident leadership. This, no doubt, explains the rise of dictatorships, but a coxswain's tyranny is at least a benevolent one, By handling decisions like setting the course, the cox frees the rowers' energies for more immediate tasks. But for this to work, the crew must have faith in the steersman, must believe in the course they are on." - (Mind Over Water)

Chapter 1
Terms

Being familiar with the sport you are in, and the shell you are commanding is an essential element to being a coxswain. This is the first step to gaining assumed competency from your rowers and from your coach. Everyone has to start somewhere, and knowing the difference between port and starboard is a good start.

Coxswain (cox-in) - A relatively small person sitting in the stern of the shell who steers, gives calls to the crew, and passes along directions from the coach to the crew.

Alternative definitions (via urbandictionary.com) that I encourage you to read because they are quite amusing.

Coxswain - the very tiny yet powerful person that steers and directs their boat on a crew team.
The coxswain is the embodiment of their coach, often referred to as the "coaches' minion". they have a weird

relationship with their coach that doesn't exist between rowers and coaches. coxswains out in the real world can be identified by a peculiar tan line in the middle of their forehead from the nk strap attached to their coxbox, a device that amplifies their already incredibly loud voice in the boat. also sometimes called a "little tyrant", coxswains are in control of everything that happens in and around their boat. unfortunately, this means they must also take complete responsibility for any damage to the boat, even if it isn't their fault. a good coxswain can make their boat move faster than that boat is generally physically able to move. don't ask how, its a coxswain secret. another trait of a talented coxswain is to be able to criticize/fix tech in the boat without rudely calling people out. coxswains of opposing teams are often seen glaring at eachother when they are even or close in a race.

Coxswain - In crew, the small person who controls every action of rowers. Although some people would call them omnipotent gods onboard shells, they're content to be called coxswains. This person is generally more intelligent, capable, and assertive than the dumb cows pulling oars. Although the coxswain, by nature of their size and immense intellectual power, is prone to badgering and physical abuse by the much larger rowers, their job is undeniably much more crucial. Coxswains have the power to get rowers to do pretty much whatever they want, through the clever combination of coercion and being able to transition from urgent whispering to drill sergeant barking to demon-like screeching from the depths of hell.

Directions in the boat

Stern - Technically the end of the boat, where you sit

Bow - The front of the boat and where bow seat sits. This is always definable by the bow ball placed on the tip of the bow as a safety precaution

Port - (using the perspective of the coxswain) the left side of the boat

Starboard - the right side of the boat

Types of Rowing

Sweep Rowing - Each rower uses one oar on a specific side

Scull Rowing - Each rower has two oars, one on each side

Shells

<u>Shell</u> - Use either to refer to the actual boat itself

<u>Single</u> - Shell rowed by one person

<u>Pair</u> - Two person sweep rowing shell

<u>Double</u> - Two person sculling shell

<u>Four</u> - Four person sweep rowing shell

<u>Quad</u> - Four person sculling shell

<u>Eight</u> - Eight person shell

In the Shell

<u>Gunwales</u> (gun-nels) - the top outer edges of the boat. Often, rowers will complain about getting their fingers caught between the gunwale and the oar while rowing. I will agree that it is quite painful. I encourage you to sympathize.

Standards

Track - the guides that the seat rolls on. Also called the slide

Foot Stretcher - adjustable plate that the shoes are attached to

Rigger - exterior metal and removable triangle shaped attachment on the exterior of the boat that holds the oar

Oarlock- plastic part on the rigger in which the oar is placed

Ribs - run perpendicular to the keel, for structural support

Keel - runs the length of the hull, also for structural support

Oars

Shaft - straight long section of the oar

Blade - part of the oar that enters the water. Most always hatchet shaped

Handle - part of the oar you hold which may be composite or

wooden

<u>Sleeve</u> - plastic cylindrical plate that goes in the oarlock

<u>Collar</u> - plastic piece positioned around the sleeve that keeps the oar in place in the oarlock

<u>Clam</u> - a clip on plastic piece that goes against the collar to adjust the load on the oar

<u>Rowing</u>

<u>Catch</u> - The top of the stroke where the blade is first set in the water

<u>Drive</u> - Part of the stroke where the blade is pulled through the water; deriving most of its power from the rower's legs

<u>Finish</u> - The last part of the stroke where the blade comes out of the water and the legs are fully extended

<u>Recovery</u> - The part of the stroke where the rower comes

Standards

slowly up back to the catch

Feathering - Rotating the oar within the oarlock so that the blade becomes parallel to the water on the recovery and again so that it is perpendicular at the catch

Rushing - Coming up the slide too fast on the recovery causing weight to be thrown to the stern and creating the boat to momentarily lose momentum

Missing Water - Not getting the blade into the water quick enough causing one to miss the beginning of the stroke

Washing Out - Pulling the blade out of the water too soon

Skying - Going to the catch with the blade too high off the water. Caused by the handle being held too low to the gunwale

Run - The distance the boat moves while the blades are out of the water

<u>Puddles</u> - Made when the blade is pulled from the water. Pressure and run can be judged by the size of the puddles and the distance between them

<u>Crab</u> - When the oar is not pulled cleanly from the water and the blade gets stuck in the water

Chapter 2
The Coxbox

The coxbox is the all important tool for coxswains and you would probably die without it, either by your own doing, your coach's doing, or most likely your rowers' doing. Treat it as if it is your own child, it is precious. There is one other tool called the speed coach that plugs in to the boat similar to the coxbox and is supposed to tell you your boat's split time, but no body actually knows how to use it. Stick to your coxbox and know exactly how to use it. If you have the unfortunate task of having to use a speed coach, well, fake it till' you make it. This chapter strictly covers the use of the coxbox.

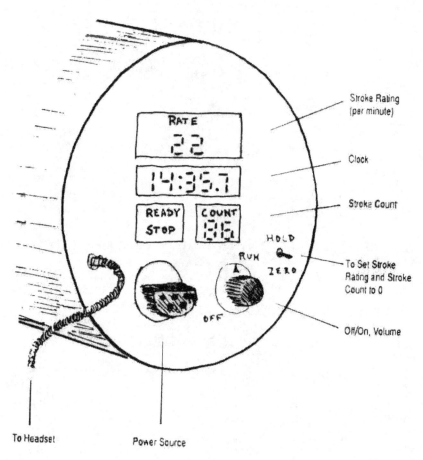

Drawing by Weir Strange

<u>On the Coxbox</u>

This is a diagram of the standard coxbox with nifty little labels that I got from google images.

You turn it on by turning the knob on the bottom to the right.

Standards

It will click. This knob also controls the volume and the more you turn it to the right, the higher the volume will be.

The rate meter tells you how many strokes per minute your rowers are taking. Your coach will ask you to keep your rowers at a certain stroke rating for pieces and races so this is very important.

The stroke count does exactly what it sounds like it would do. It counts strokes. As long as the timer is going it will count strokes.

The microphone plugs into the microphone socket. For this model it spins into a lock position. For the newer ones it just plugs in.

To clear the timer and restart it you hold down the toggle until it goes to 0 on the timer and stroke count. To pause the timer and stroke count click the toggle down once, and to start it again, click it down once more.

There is a wire in the boats that plug into the power

connection on the coxbox. Needless to say, this is how you connect the coxbox to the boat as well as to its charger.

You also need to keep the coxboxes clean. Your coach should instruct you on how to do this, and you will need to do it every couple months or however frequently you are instructed to do so. There is a lubricant that you put in the connection areas. You also should take something with a narrow but sharp point and clean out any dirt build up around the edges.

Always be responsible for your coxbox. It is not the varsity's job to pack your coxbox for races, nor is it the varsity's job to bring an extra coxbox in the case that you forget.

The Ticks

My team has some pretty old coxboxes that have their own "personalities," and even the newer ones are displaying some of their own interesting traits. Some of the older ones you have to turn upside down in the coxswain hole to get them working. You also may have to place the speaker connection and the plug for the boat in the saltwater to get the speakers working in the boat. There is also a nasty little tip I can offer. For the newer coxboxes, if the speakers are not working, you can spit into the headset connection as well as the boat plug in to help connection.

In Conclusion

Coxboxes are extremely important to the job. they are the main tools by which we can do our work. They help us communicate, and coach while on the water. They also cost about $600 so take good care of them.

Loryn Schopke

The coxswain seat in an eight

Chapter 3
Basics of Steering

One responsibility you have is to steer the shell. It is one of the many parts of your balancing act on the water. Fairly easy to do, but very difficult to master, steering has been ranked second in importance among the list of what is looked for in a coxswain. The shells you steer are the eights and the fours which both have their pros and cons.

Eights

Eights are pretty easy to steer in concept. You have ropes on either side of the gunwale in the coxswain seat as shown in the picture. To steer starboard (to the right), you simply push the right side of the rope forward, and to steer port (towards the left) you push the left side of the rope forward.

- The main pros to steering an eight include the fact that they are easier to steer in a straight line due to the slow responsiveness of the rudder, and the fact that you can see your rowers and comment on any problems you see and can fix.

- The main cons include the big blind spot you have directly in front of you where your giant stroke seat sits. One time, another boat was coming at my boat and we happened to both be in each other's blind spots and we ran head on, right into each other. So, as a general rule, **always check your blind spot.** It's just like driving a car in that regard. Another con is the fact that they are fairly difficult to turn because they are so long and not very responsive.

Turning:

Remember it takes about 4 to 5 strokes for the boat to even start responding, so, when turning, take the boat wide first and then hit the rudder early. You have to remember to turn with your bow and not your stern, meaning that you need to use your bow as a reference point versus your position in the stern because it is about 60 feet from you.

<u>Fours</u>

The difficult thing about fours at first is the fact that there are two different types of fours and three different types of steering in fours. There are stern loaded fours, and bow loaded fours. By "loaded," I mean where the coxswain sits. So in stern loaded fours, the coxswain sits in the stern, and in bow loaded fours the coxswain is loaded into the bow. I don't really have much experience with stern loaded fours and personally I think they're pretty basic and lame. I can only take a shot in the dark and say that they probably are steered like eights, only more responsive because they are shorter.

Bow Loaded Fours

Bow loaded fours get their own section because I have quite a bit of experience with them. There are two different types of steering in fours that the coxswains on my team like to call the "popsicle," and the "throttle,"

Popsicle Steering - There is a stick right in front of your face that looks like a popsicle stick (hence the name popsicle steering) and if you push it to the right then you will go right and if you push it to the left you will go left. This one is pretty simple to understand. Just know that these boats are a lot more responsive than the eights so you don't need to push it all the way to either side unless you are taking a very sharp turn.

Throttle Steering - On the right side of the coxswain hole there is a device that looks like a throttle, (hence the name throttle steering). To go right, you push the throttle forward, and to go left, you pull it backwards. This one you will just need to practice with in order to remember. By the way, the boat will not go faster if you push the throttle forward. It will just go right.

Generally fours are fairly easy to turn in so I really wouldn't worry about that.

<u>Spinning</u>

By "spinning," I am referring to turning the boat around, and there are two methods to doing this. Neither one has been proven to be more effective one just looks cleaner.

- First, you can have all of your ports row and your starboards back or vice versa
- Alternatively, in an eight, you can have 8 and 6 seat row and 1 and 3 seat back or vice versa
- In a four, have 4 seat row and bow seat back, or vice versa

As a tip try to spin towards the shore in most situations, as it is generally more protected from wind and choppy water by the shore.

<u>**Conclusion**</u>

When it comes to steering, you will just have to get a feel for it. It is helpful to know a few shortcuts and tips, but it will mostly be up to you to get used to. So when you get tossed out in an eight with little to no instruction on how to steer it , don't panic and just play around with it. I have been advised in so many different ways about how to steer a straight line and none of them have worked for me in all honesty. I will leave it up to you to figure that one out. Please do so in a timely manner though because no one will take you seriously until you can steer a decently straight line.

Chapter 4
Basic Calls

Of course, I understand that each coxswain calls things differently and that is ok, but it does need to be coherent. I hear coxswains making calls for the simplest of actions and there are times when I cant make sense out of what they're saying and then I ask myself, "if they can't call a boat out of slings what happens during a race?" Honestly it terrifies and slightly amuses me, so to avoid being mocked by other coxswains, (which happens quite frequently), here are some basic calls.

Loryn Schopke

Call Definitions

<u>All eight</u> - Called when a boat is not all rowing, either because of a drill or warm up. Usually rowers are given two strokes to prepare. So, "In two, all eight"

<u>Back it down</u> - Usually with stern pair or four, a call made to move the boat backwards when moving out of the way or backing into a stake boat or dock for racing

<u>Check it down</u> - having all eight rowers square up their blades in the water to stop quickly

<u>Easy</u> - Call made to lessen the pressure rowers are using

<u>Easy on port/starboard</u> - Call made to lessen the pressure on one side in order to turn

<u>Hands on</u> - Lets the rowers know to be prepared to lift up the boat together

<u>Hard on port/starboard</u> - Call made to increase pressure on

one side in order to turn

<u>Heads up</u> - Call made to let people know a boat is coming through the area

<u>High 10</u> - Call made in the beginning of a race for rowers to make 10 strokes at a very high rating

<u>Hold Water</u> - Having the rowers square up their blades in the water to keep the shell from drifting

<u>In two</u> - For calling changed while rowing. The coxswain should give the rowers two strokes notice before changing anything about changing rating, drills, pairs or anything else

<u>Let it run</u> - Having the rowers stop rowing but allowing the momentum of the boat to continue

<u>On the feather</u> - Calling the rowers to row while feathering their blade

<u>On the square</u> - Calling the rowers to row while keeping their

blade on the square

<u>On this one</u> - Call made as a transition into a piece or new drill to let rowers know that they have transitioned

<u>Paddle</u> - Telling the rowers to row with light pressure

<u>Power 10</u> - Call made during a race or piece where the rowers take 10 strokes at a very high pressure to increase speed as an attack call.

<u>Set the boat</u> - Call made when the boat is leaning to either side. Mostly notifying bow pair, but the entire boat is also responsible

<u>Sit ready</u> - Tells rowers to move to the catch or ¾ slide position to be ready to start a piece or race

<u>Settle</u> - Called during a race to bring the crew down to their base race rating after a the initial high 10

<u>Scull</u> - Call made at the starting line to reposition the bow of

your boat.

<u>Spin it</u> - Call made to turn the boat around

<u>Up to waist ready up</u> - call made telling the rowers to lift the boat up to waist level

<u>Up over heads ready up</u> - telling rowers to lift the boat up over heads

<u>Down to shoulders ready down</u> - telling rowers to bring the boat down to shoulders

<u>Weigh Enough</u> - Call made to inform rowers to stop rowing. Usually followed by a call to check it down or let it run

Basic Call Processes

<u>Picking up the boat</u>

1. Hands on
2. Up to waist ready up
3. Roll over heads ready roll
4. Show (or call) sides

5. Split to shoulders ready split

If you have a boathouse

Depending on which rack the boat is on, alter the picking up the boat process as you need to

If it is on the top rack,

1. Up an inch ready up

2. Step it out

3. Show Sides

4. Split to shoulder ready split

If it is at low heads

1. Hands on

2. Up an inch ready up

3. Step it out

4. Up over heads ready up

5. Show sides

6. Split to shoulders ready split

Waist level

Standards

1. Hands on

2. Up an inch ready up

3. Step it out

4. Split under (two from each end in an 8, one from each end in a 4)

On wheels

1. Hands on

2. Roll it out

3. Walk around

NEVER step over the shell

4. Hands on

5. Up to waist ready up, up to shoulders ready up

Dock Launching

if it is a long wait let them go to waist level, they will love you

make sure you go down bow first

1. Walk it down, up over heads as you go down

2. Weigh enough

3. Toes to the edge

4. Roll down to waist, ready roll

5. Out (meaning out away from the dock), and in

Wet Launching

this is just launching without a dock and walking the boat directly into the water

The process is pretty much the same as dock launching only without steps 3 and the first half of 5. Just walk the boat bow first straight out into the water and walk far enough to **clear the skeg** from hitting mud or sand in the water.

Make sure that when you are walking with your boat walk with the bow and always keep an eye on the stern

Once the shell is on the water

Push off and immediately get your point. My team has to row through a narrow canal once we launch and the first thing we have to do is have bow seat take a stroke.

Have bow four or stern four row to give the other four time to get strapped in and then switch.

Chapter 5

On The Water Practices

Practices on the water are, in my opinion and also in my rowers' opinions, the best practices. They are also probably the most crucial, because, as it is commonly said, ergs do not float. You are as crucial to the running of these practices as the coach is and it is hugely important to be competent and know what you're doing.

Loryn Schopke

Cardinal Directions

So, generally in any water sport or water related activity, you're going to want to know your cardinal directions. I have my own mental compass based on my boathouse's location which is conveniently next to the beach.

North is toward Mather's bridge and Pineda Causeway
South is toward Dragon Point
East is toward the beach
West is toward mainland

Of course these will not work for everyone, but I highly suggest you come up with your own mental compass. You will sometimes be told to take your crew in a certain direction or have to decide which side of the body of water you need to be on based on the wind and it helps to know where exactly you are going. Plus you get competency points.

Flow of Traffic

I will cover this more later in the context of racing, but the body of water you are on will always have a flow of traffic just like roads do. Generally, these are the rules of the flow of traffic

- Keep to the right side of the body of water
- Our shells have the right of way over other boats
- Also, never go under the left side of any bridge because this is America and we go under the right side of the bridge. If you don't you're a communist

Listen to instruction

The most important things here, in order, are to listen to your coach and be completely aware of your surroundings

Often, it is really difficult to hear your coach while on the water, and sometimes you will get lucky, but most of the time you can't gt away with not having heard them. Drills work is done to work on the rowers' technique and the individual drills can get pretty complicated to remember and then properly execute, but they are extremely important. I hate

41

doing it, but the best way to avoid messing up drills or missing instruction is to ask coach. Of course you can probably ask your rowers but you risk a slight loss of confidence if you go that route. You can usually avoid all of this by just listening intently, as it is one of your jobs.

Communication

This section is important for a couple of reasons. The first pertains to the other coxswains on the water with you, as there is generally at least one. Your coach will want to coach both boats, hence them both being out there. This means that in order to keep them together you have to talk to each other. Coxswains that work well together make practice go way more efficiently, than coxswains that don't. You will want to talk to them about:

- **Your point** - It's difficult to keep boats together when neither one of them are aware of where the other intends to be pointed. You will either end up three lanes apart, or one of you will find yourselves snaking all over the place trying to follow a mystery point. Before you start rowing, just either tell them where you intend to be pointed, or ask them if they would like to point in the same direction, which is more polite. Also, if you are going through a curve around the land then communicate on when you would like to straighten out your point. At times, you may be dealing with a coxswain less experienced than you, in which case they will probably be looking to you to guide them so hold to your line and simply tell them where you are intending to point so that they can follow.

- **The drills** - Your coach may tell you to complete a certain drill by sixes or pairs, or pausing, and then to take it away by all eight continuous. Again, you are expected to keep the boats fairly close, which is impossible if one coxswain takes their boat by all eight and the other is still finishing the drill. This one is pretty simple, just ask the other coxswain to let you know when they are ready to go all eight.

You will also need to communicate with your rowers. It helps everyone a great deal if you are talking to them. You both have different perspectives on the shell. The rower knows the stroke and how the pieces feel to them, while the coxswain knows how they look. You act as the coach within the shell, which is why there's a whole chapter on the technique of the stroke you thought was irrelevant because you don't row. You should also ask them their opinions on what they think needs to be done to improve the boat.

Getting off the water

You are also in charge of this aspect of water practices and this is really where you need to be forceful and firm in your instructions in order to maintain their focus because at this point your rowers want to go home. Make sure that your rowers stay quiet and attentive if you have a difficult docking job like my team does at the end of the day. Also, dock using your stern pair.

- Try to be as parallel to the dock as possible. If you approach at a sharp angle, things get difficult and you look dumb.

- Slow down! Everyone wants to get off the dock, but don't come flying in like a moron. You will break something.

Standards

Make sure that people are washing the shell, getting oars put away, and not wasting time once you are on land.

In Conclusion

Water practices are essential to the success of the team and you have the potential to make or break a practice. No pressure. This is where we, as coxswains can get some recognition from our rowers and build a relationship with our coaches so take the time to engage with them in a productive manner and allow yourself to learn, and build yourself up as a leader.

Chapter 6
Technique of the Stroke

One of the coxswain's responsibilities is to work with the rowers on the technique of the stroke. This makes it especially important for a coxswain to understand the technique of the stroke despite the fact that we don't row. Your coach will not be able to constantly remind the rowers about what they need to work on as a boat and individually nor will he/she want to. The coaches will want to give everything they purpose and importance and so they should. If they are constantly making technical comments to each rower then they will eventually be ignored and drowned out. So this task falls on the coxswains. It is our job to constantly be making corrections while making sure that we will not be eventually ignored. This overview of the technique of the stroke was written by Coach Ethan and is fairly detailed, but it is all important for you to understand. Key ideas are bolded.

Standards

The technical aspect of our approach to rowing, though not a trade secret, should not be something you as a member of our program should be readily sharing with other teams. We do not want other programs to understand how we row and how we approach our rowing from an internal standpoint.

The coxswain's job is to first ensure safety, second ensure the best context for racing and third to motivate and "coach" the rowers. By ensuring the best context the reader should understand this to mean that the coxswain should always be perceptive and aware of their surroundings, the weather and other shells and place their crew and shell in the best position physically to perform their best. In terms of coaching the stroke, the coxswain is the only person on race day that can adequately ensure the rowers are rowing with a technical aptitude that is acceptable. Therefore, understand the rowing stroke, the physics of the shell through the water and the style that we here at Space Coast Crew are looking for is critical to the position of coxswain.

The stroke step by step

Starting at the finish position, the rowers should begin the recovery of their stroke by reaching the arms forward and then the body.

Before a rower's legs begin to compress they must have at least ¾ of their upper-body position in place, meaning that the **rower should almost entirely be reaching into the catch with their upper body before their legs follow**.

- Ideally, we would like rowers to maintain their shoulders over their thighs at almost all points during the rowing stroke.

The rowers should begin the upper body movements nearly, but not entirely simultaneously, with the hands (**moving slightly before** the upper body).

- The entire motion of the upper body moving through the recovery should be smooth and fluid.

The hands should come away from the body in a downward motion (**making somewhat of a "C"**) and should continue down until their outside hand is approximately 3 inches above the gunwale, or as their leg size permits.

- Once in this position is achieved the oars will look nearly **parallel with the level of the shell**, or beyond.

Standards

The rowers then begin to compress their legs in a single motion. As the rowers compress their seats towards the catch their wrists should begin lifting into the catch as they **slowly** square their blades. At ¾ slide the rowers should be nearly **entirely square** with almost no further motion needed towards that end.

- The bottom edge of the blade should now be within inches of the water's surface the shoulders should be relaxed and rotated evenly towards their riggers.

From ¾ slide compression forward the rowers should be squared and begin lifting their hands to drop the blade into the water. As the rowers finish their recovery on the slide they should be **"backing" their blades into the water**. The ideal catch should show an equal amount of water being splashed both forwards and backwards around the blade. This is called the v-splash.

The rowers, having locked their blade into the catch position in the water now, should immediately fire their legs back to flat and allow their backs to straighten as they drive, but should not stretch their backs like a rubber band. 90% of all effort exerted during the drive phase of the rowing stroke should take place before half slide when the blade is perpendicular to the shell. **Their upper bodies should not initiate any pulling motion until the legs are nearly completely extended.** Only then should the rowers swing their backs towards the bow in a smooth and continuous motion and only with the intention of maintaining pressure on the blade face which was built up with the legs.

- When the rowers have driven their legs to 2/3 of the length of the slides their shoulders should, by that point, be directly over their hips.

At the finish the rowers should pull the **handle all the way into their lower ribs** and nearly touch their skin with the handle before pushing the handle down. While lifting the blade from the water the hands should return to a cocked position feathering the blade out.

- The coxswain here should take note to ensure that the rowers do not lift water out when they are lifting their blades from the water. Water carried out of the finish will spray towards the stern when they feather and is a symptom of feathering too soon at the finish.

The rowers shoulders should be relaxed, their hands should be hanging, but not gripping the oar, and their chests should be expanded. Their backs should be mostly straight, but not rigid. **It is only at this moment that the rower's shoulders are behind their hips**.

The Physics of the Rowing Stroke

The coxswain should always be aware that a rudder in a rowing shell is ineffective for rapid and spontaneous adjustments to the course. The hull is long and straight and resists any movement that is not linear forwards. Coxswains should also note that a fully rigged and manned rowing shell will weigh **approximately two-thirds to three-fourths of a ton, or 1700 lbs. The shell is moving the fastest immediately after the blades have exited the water at the finish and the slowest just before the drive during the stroke.**

The rowing 8, with the multiple long oars, exaggerated length and weight and shape requires a particular motion from the rowers to utilize its qualities for speed. When the blades are in the catch position the handles do not move perfectly toward the bow and thus the shell is pinched through the act of driving the legs. When the blades are at the finish they are again not perpendicular with the shell and this creates an expanding action on the shell itself. This squeeze and stretch of the gunwales of the 8 create an ever changing hull shape and lost energy. Therefore, in order to utilize the oars for driving the shell through the water when they are at their peak efficiency the rowers must apply the most pressure on the blade when the oar is passing though the **perpendicular point of the stroke (when the oar is perfectly perpendicular to the boat).** This point is referred to as "through the pin" because the rower's hips are passing past the point of the pin in the rigger.

However, because the rowing shell is heavy with all of its equipment and rowers, it is necessary for the rowers to build acceleration in their drive before they reach the perpendicular point, or through the pin. Furthermore, because the shell rapidly squeezes at the catch, the friction with the water is reduced and therefore the shell can slip through the water more effectively at this point. All of these points combined mean that **the rowers should concentrate on driving their legs the hardest in the top 6-8 inches of the slide while they are the most compressed.**

For the coxswain, the rowing stroke in the 8 should feel forceful and impulsive in terms of power application at the catch, but fluid and accelerated at the finish.

Standards

The coxswain **must lean forward in their seat constantly** and allow the boat to surge under them without being thrown either forwards or backwards. The coxswain must move fluidly with the shell and not allow his or her body to be thrown in order to not become a hindrance to the boat movement through the water.

A lot if this is fairly complex and you may want to refer to it as you become more advanced as a coxswain and gain experience and understanding about the shells and how they should feel to you during a row. It is important to have this in writing for you because, unless you have had experience as a rower, you will not understand the technique of the stroke as well as a coxswain who has. The rowers will be expecting you to comment about their technique and assist them in correcting any flaws they have. This ability will gain you respect from your rowers and your coach so make sure you have a fair understanding of the stroke.

Chapter 6
Land Practices

Land practices are nearly if not as essential as water practices. The coach gets to work closely with individual rowers if need be, and the teams can get "swole". It may seem like a day that coxswains do nothing, but that is quite the contrary. We can do a lot during these practices, and I encourage you to not be the lazy, pint sized wastes of space on land days.

Ergometer Workouts

No, we do not participate in these (we're not all that upset about it), but you don't just stand there and talk and laugh and watch your rowers suffer on these death machines. This is an opportunity for you to a) become familiar with each of your rower's individual techniques b) become familiar with technique in general c) work closely with your rowers and comment on what you think they need to fix and what they are doing well with. I also would like to say that as a previous rower, I can say that I HATE it when people are just standing behind ergs and talking and making noise so don't do it. Ever. (technically we can erg if we really want to and if that is what you want to do, I think you're being an idiot, but that is your decision).

Lifting/ Running

We can indeed participate in these (except me because I hate running and find it to be pointless unless faced with eminent diabetes or death by an advancing attacker). Let me tell you though, if you do you will gain massive respect points from your rowers. So, I suggest you do participate in these workouts. However, before you make your decision ask your coach if he needs anything from you for the workout, like recording certain information or cleaning coxboxes while they are not in use.

Be Available

Do all the tedious menial tasks that no one wants to do, mostly because it is helpful, but also to gain some brownie points with your coach/rowers because we all know there's always an ulterior motive to most things in general. Things like

- clean the ergs
- put them away
- put weights/ medicine balls away
- clean the boathouse (sweep, organize etc.)
- check down the boats
- attend to the coaches every request
- Do not be in the way

And also be available to answer any questions that the rowers have and try your hardest to know the answer. If you don't know, don't lie about it, just find the answer.

In Conclusion

We as coxswains are not expected to do much on land day practices, but when we do it's like a breath of fresh air to our coaches and our rowers. On top of keeping ourselves in shape and at a healthy weight, it shows that we respect our rowers work enough to do it ourselves, and that we do not place ourselves above it. Believe me when I say that the tests and workouts that these rowers put themselves through are brutal. I know it, because I've done it. It is hard work, and to place yourself right there next to them when you do not have to means more than you can understand.

Chapter 7
Basics of Races

There is a lot to know about races and there is a lot that we are responsible for on race days especially. We are expected to remember everything because ultimately we are responsible for getting our boats on and off the water. Regatta days are what we train for so it is very important to be prepared so as not to make a mistake. This is where we display the leadership we are building and show how competent we can be. It is stressful, and overwhelming, but have fun though, because the payoff to winning a race is completely worth it for everyone.

Standards

<u>Types of Racing</u>

Generally, high school rowing teams will participate in two different types of racing: head racing and sprint racing.

Head Races - These races are considered fall/winter races as that is the time frame during which they are held. These races are 5ks (5000 meters or about 3.1 miles) give or take, depending on the course. They are raced individually and against the clock. An official will start each individual boat's time and their objective is to pass the boat in front of them, which would assure that you have beaten that boat's time, if they are in your event. The general rules (my rules as well as official rules) are as follows

- These are long races so do not take them at a stroke rating of 35. The rowers will probably die.
- They are usually around 15-20 minutes
- When there are bridges on the course you are generally not allowed to pass under them, mostly because there will usually be no room.
- When you are about to pass a boat you turn your

59

volume up and yell to the coxswain of said shell "Coxswain Yield!" and they should move to give you the shorter course.

- The inside of the course is the shorter course. Whichever turns are tighter etc.

- Just because the course is not in a straight line does not mean that you can swerve all over the place. Pick a course and stick to it or you'll look like an imbecile on top of adding time to your final score. Using the rudder adds drag and therefore causes the boat to become heavier to pull.

- Do not just call power 10s. This goes for sprint racing too. Your rowers will ignore you. Every call you make should have some sort of purpose. I hate power 10s. They are for weak minded people rowers and coxswains alike. You can still use them, just tread wisely.

- If a coxswain is dumb and can't follow simple rules of racing and happens to hinder your race, then you can protest and make them lose, but you must do so on the water or it will not count. Make sure you have a good reason for it as well because it costs money.

Relevant Race 1) Jacksonville Head Race

Obviously in Jacksonville, Florida, this race is known for its bridges, sharpish turn, and poor water conditions. You start off going through a "shoot" that allows you to build up to race pace, because you row into the race itself. The course is winding starting with a wide left turn. The you will hit a bridge and then another bridge (you are technically not allowed to pass in the area in between these two bridges but I have done it every year so don't take it too seriously). Then after the second bridge there will be a sharpish right turn and then the finish line like 1000 meters later. Do not go through the bridge at the very end. I suggest that you address your coach on practicing turns especially if you are in eights.

Relevant Race 2) Head of the Hooch :)

This is my favorite race of the season because I get to go to Tennessee and spend all weekend with my favorite people on the face of the planet and race on a beautiful and perfectly run course. It is cold a.f. so buy a multitude of layers so you can marshmallow up and be warmer than everyone. This race is huge and I respect it a lot so you need to follow the rules of this race explicitly.

- Wear a watch - you will likely not be able to find your coach considering the vastness of the venue so you will need to know what time your race is and what time you are launching.

- There are no turns really, the course is just one large curve. There are two bridges that they say you cannot pass under, but you can totally fit at least three boats under it so don't even be concerned. I would suggest you somewhat consider avoiding it.

- Be very aware of the dock, both launching and docking procedures. Listen very closely to the officials. I like them, they are the only nice officials that are actually officials. Once you are on the dock give yourself no more than 45 seconds and then get off of it and get away from it. Have one four/pair row and then switch to the other pair so that they can strap in. When docking, again, listen to the officials on which dock to go to. Then get off of it as soon as possible and follow their instructions on where to take your shell.

- Follow the traffic pattern and try to stay within range of your bow number. If your bow number is number 200 then stick with boats 190-210.

Sprint Racing - Sprint races are considered spring races because they are done in the spring/ summer ish time of the year, depending on where you live. They are generally 1500 meters if you live in Florida, and 2000 meters everywhere else. There are way more sprint races than head races because they are short, lasting at most 6-7 minutes if you row with women. You are either held at the start line side by side by launches called stake-boats, or you float side by side in what is called a floating start, or you are held side by side on the line by people on something called a stake dock. You are all started at the same time and race against each other versus racing against the clock like you do in head races. The most important things to remember about sprint races are :

- Stay in your lane
- Do not lane hop or leave your lane
- Do not run into someone else that is not in your lane therefore rendering you out of your lane
- Listen to officials

- Call the Sprint
- Stay in your lane
- Do not call 15 power tens, because NO ONE will like that

There is an extremely simple outline of the race plan for a sprint race and it is

- Start Sequence
- Middle Move
- Sprint

Anything else in between is up to you and your boat, but mostly you. The race plan changes based on what is happening in the race. If the boat next to you is calling a move, then you better call a counter move. If you are in the lead, call something to open up the gap. If you are in last place, then call something to get them through it. There is no fool proof race plan, there is just strategic and adaptable coxing.

Chapter 8

Basics of Race Day

Race day involves a lot of little things that are essential to remember. This chapter is essentially a list of things to do on race day, but it needs to be emphasized. Being on top of things on race day will prove to your coach that you can be on top of things all the time, as race days are high stress situations for us coxswains. Remember more than your basic responsibilities. Be prepared for everything any anything.

The Coaches/Coxswains Meeting

The first part of your day is the coaches and coxswains meeting where the officials of the regatta call together all the coaches and the coxswains from all of the teams and talks about the plan for the day as far as racing schedule, and course overview. Pay attention to mostly:

- The traffic pattern
- Regatta time - the officials will have a certain watch or clock that they will base time off of. It is suggestible to sync your own watch to this time
- Weather predictions for the day
- First Aid locations

Make note of all of these and whatever other information you find to be pertinent to the particular race.

Your fanny pack

No they are not just for tourists. These bags are convenient little portable tool kits that every coxswain should have. You should include:

- a 7/16ths wrench
- a 3/4s wrench
- a coxswain tool (it has a wing nut wrench)
- spare spacers
- medical tape
- band aids (water proof)
- Neosporin

Your Own Preparation (this is what I do)

1. Check the race schedule in order to determine the time of your race and who is in your race because the rowers will want to know.
2. Ask your coach what time he thinks is most appropriate to round up your rowers, as well as what bow number you are so you can attach the correct number. (You can be disqualified or penalized if you have the wrong bow number or an improper bow number).
3. Check down your shell hours before your race. Check the following.
    a. The riggers of the boat - go through each rigger

with a 7/16ths wrench and a 3/4s wrench and make sure each rigger is tightened properly.

b. The speakers - simply plug in your coxbox and headset and do a sound check on the speakers on the boat to make sure that all of them work.

c. The seats - Check the wheels to make sure that none of them are cracked and the tracks to make sure that the seats are not sticking.

d. The heel ties - The heels of the shoes are tied down to the base of the plate as a safety measure. Make sure each shoe is tied down to the plate, leaving room for the heel to come up enough for the rower to give pressure.

e. The steering - Make sure that the steering on the shell is working and that the skeg is maneuvering properly.

f. The bow ball - Simply make sure that the bow ball is attached securely as well as the bow number.

4. Make sure that you know where your oars are/ what oar set you are using/ there are people to carry your oars to your rowers.

5. In regards to your crew

    a. Make sure you have water bottles for your rowers.

    b. Have inhalers if need be

    c. SUNSCREEN THEM ALL - I don't care if they want it or not.

6. Talk to your rowers through

    a. What to expect - make sure that they know you are in charge and that you know what you are doing.

    b. The race plan - no matter how simple it is and if it simply is to carry out your every command without question

    c. Give them a pep talk and place them in the proper state of mind for the race. Remember that they are the ones pulling you across the finish line.

Getting to the start

You do not just row up to the start and then go. We like to keep things as complex as unnecessary. So, when rowing up to the start:

1. Follow a warm up plan as well as the traffic pattern for the warm up area. This may consist of various drills, or 10s along side of the course.
2. Stop rowing when a race is going by, as it is respectful.
3. While waiting to be called to the start, have your rowers check their oarlocks/ spacers/ slide/ foot plate position.
4. Be wary of instructions by the officials in the launches. They will call you to the start by your lane number in order.

When backing into the stake boats or docks or simply to a floating start - Use your stern pair or four, do not move the skeg from the equilibrium point, and have various sides give pressure as needed.

When getting your point you will need to skull if you have stake boats/ a dock and for a floating start you will need to play around with it in response to the wind (have your bow pointed slightly into the wind if possible). To skull have your two seat take small arms only strokes with bow seat's oarto move the bow to the left, or have your three seat take arms only strokes with two seat's oar to move the bow to the right.

The Race (what to say and when):

The Start - Each start is different, but most have a few starting strokes, followed by a number of high rating, high intensity strokes, and then a number of lengthening, settle strokes. These are called however the crew prefers them to be called, which makes comunication important.

On location - It is suggestible to tell your crew the position of every other crew in your race. Go down the lanes first and tell them where each boat is in the race. Then, from that point on, tell them only where the two closest boats are to you, one in front and one behind or in accordance to where you are.

The plan - As I have mentioned before, there is no set race plan usually. It always changes. You need to be aware of what needs to happen to reach the next boat or to put distance in between you and the boat behind you.

<u>The Middle</u> - This is where many crews make a big move, either to break through the half way barrier and start out strong in the second half, or to attack/ defend a position. 10s are thrown right and left, it is up to you to decide what your crew needs at the half way point. Do not be afraid to make a ballsy move and call three 10s at half way because you are neck and neck with another crew.

<u>If the boat is falling apart</u> - You can call focuses in the form of 10s or individual strokes. You can focus on finding the problem: catch/finish timing, ratio, power curve location, handle heights etc., and call it out.

<u>If the boat is rowing well together</u> - Keep the focus on putting distance between you and the other crews. Keep your rowers listening to you, do not say mindless things just to fill up silence. Do not be afraid to call them out by name, encourage them to give more, and to do more. Keep them alert and confident and strong even in extreme exhaustion.

Standards

<u>The Finish</u> - This is the last chance you have to change the outcome of the race. It is important to remember calling the sprint.

- Do not feel pressured to sprint at a certain location on the meter mark, if you are behind then sprint early, (never before the 400 meter mark at the most) and if you are ahead then you are allowed to be slightly late.

- Be aggressive especially in this part of the race, as before the rowers needed you to talk out what is happening in the race, and now they need the push to pull harder than before.

- Do not lose control, or else everything falls apart.

- Do not force a rating on a crew that they cannot handle. Keep it manageable.

- The last 10 strokes are important to rowers and it is better to call them late than early. There is nothing worse than calling your last 10 strokes and then having to call a few more after that.

- When you cross the finish line DO NOT let your rowers collapse and look completely dead.

LOOK GOOD. You want to look like nothing happened, like you were just steady state rowing. It shows strength and confidence and finesse. A sign of a good crew.

Chapter 9
Motivation

Coaches get quiet about their teams individual team rowing style that they teach, and coxswains get quiet about their individual motivation techniques. Even when not competing against each other, coxswains like to keep these things to themselves. It is a pride thing. However, there are some motivation tips that are universal and well known by all experienced coxswains.

There is a multitude of things you can say so let us begin with what you should not say.

- Avoid frequent repetition. This is the quickest way to be sure that you are quickly tuned out and ignored

- Do not make the entire race a power 10 it is extremely ineffective and stupid.

- Unless it is requested by your rowers, I would suggest avoiding giving them calls of distance in regards to where they lay in the race. Only in regards to other boats should you speak of distance and speak only in measurements of seats and boatlengths.

- Avoid being a cheerleader. This sport is aggressive and you must act as such.

- Avoid being the little king in the stern of the shell and slave drive your rowers to victory. You are not above them. Be one of them an they will likely pull for you, therefore giving them another reason to pull and therefore making them faster.

- Do not say things for no reason. Have a purpose behind your words. Make calls and tell them why you are making them. Include them in your reasoning and they will be more willing to carry out your call.

Standards

- Do not just yell violently and lose control, you just look stupid. Control your volume with what is appropriate for the moment. The recovery should be far more controlled than the drive. The drive is aggressive and violent.

As far as what you should say, there are a few consistent calls that coxswains tend to make

- The individual words "push," and "drive," make for excellent fillers if you are at a loss for words. Do not overuse them though, they lose their effectiveness.

- Always explain to them what they need to do next, and what it will take to get there. For example, if you are wanting to start walking past a boat, tell them that they need to attack these strokes and pass each seat in that shell, one at a time. Tell them which seat they are on, and tell them to take the next seat.

- Use focus calls. You can isolate a certain part of the stroke, namely the leg drive, catch time, and length and have them focus on that.

- For phrases you can use, I would suggest looking up various motivational quotes and taking bits and pieces from there. I would also pay attention to what other coxswains are saying and using.

Every crew is motivated differently and this is why this chapter is shorter than one would expect. Some rowers are motivated by male aggression, some by female aggression, some need logic, and some need mere volume alone. It is your job to communicate with your rowers so that you can identify what they prefer, and determine what also works best for them as a boat. If what you're saying wouldn't motivate you, then chances are it won't motivate them either. It is a trial and error process on just what to say for each shell, and you have to work with each one to find it.

Chapter 10
Line ups

These cause the most conflicts and bad blood between coxswains. Line ups stress the coxswains probably more than it does the rowers. There is only one seat to fight for per boat so it is all or nothing in most cases. Not only are we fighting to be in the boats, but once we are in them, we fight to bring them together. Certain line ups come with a stigma, an image, of what it means to the team and the coach. Line ups are complicated, but we simply cannot race and win by throwing random rowers in random seats with random coxswains. It is like being in a sort of blended family, being that you cannot always choose who rows with you, but it is your job to make sure that whichever rowers you are coxing for are rowing for you, and for each other.

Loryn Schopke

The fight - First thing is first, you have to make it in to the shell. There are other coxswains fighting for a seat in the boat so this will not be easy. You can approach this one of two ways. You can observe every and all things you see the other coxswains do and the effect it has on the rowers as well as look up coxing videos and tips on the Internet: learning by imitation. Or, you can develop yourself as a coxswain by yourself for yourself for the team: learn by experience. The combination of both is probably the most effective, but I do find that coxswains tend to fall to one side or the other. You shouldn't play dirty, nor should you be outwardly intolerant of a coxswain that beat you, or is after your seat. Keep your biases to yourself. Talk to the coach, but not in excess. Speak to him/her on what he/she would like to see more of, specifically from you if you can manage to get that answer. These line up fights are not always fair, but are always intense, and while you are fighting for your stance on the team you are expected to maintain an air of confidence, and professionalism. What is most essential, when all is said and done, is for you to put your full effort and complete dedication into the lineup you are placed in.

Standards

First Varsity vs. Second Varsity vs. Third Varsity/Novice - These three categories are what you will have to deal with most often on the team. There is a definite separation between the three boats that grows with decreasing levels of competitiveness.

The 1v, or first varsity, seems to get the majority of the coach's attention and effort being that it is the most competitive boat on the team. These rowers are on top; they are the fastest and are usually all business all the time. As a novice, you will likely not see this boat for at least a year or two, but it is important to recognize and be familiar with the general boat personality type that seems to take hold in the 1v. Look at this shell as if you will be in it some day, not as something largely and permanently out of your league as a coxswain, because I promise you it is not.

The 2v or the second varsity, is something entirely different and is something I personally know quite a lot about. Coxing the 2v places one in an interesting position. The 2v has a tendency of developing a sort of complex. Half of its rowers are fighting for a seat in the 1v and the other half are struggling to stay out of the 3v. As a result, you have a spilt minded boat, and a boat/event that rarely gets its own focus. As the coxswain of the 2v it is your job to bring this motley group together. If not to be satisfied with the shell they are placed in, because that cannot be asked, to row for the common purpose of making the boat as fast as possible. Of course there will always be ulterior motives among the crew, but it is your job to discover these motives and make them applicable to the cause of the boat.

The 3v is generally a novice boat. The novice category is one that is becoming less and less popular so this boat is primarily one that is used to train rowers for the 2v and possibly even the 1v. Of course, they will compete in novice events if there are any, but the focus will remain on the 1 and 2v. Coxing this boat will be primarily about technique and the desire to pull.

Boat Personality

Boats will develop a sort of personality depending on their line ups and the guys in them.

I know that the boat I am in currently, which happens to be the **2v**, is an incredibly supportive and fun loving group of guys. They want respect and they want to be a part of the team, but at the same time they want something for themselves that they can be a part of. Being in the 2v they experience all the things I mentioned earlier; I have 3 or 4 of my guys struggling to fight their way into the 1v and then the rest of them rowing to stay out of the 3v at all costs. So, it makes sense for them to develop a boat personality such as the one I described.

Now the 1v, from my minimal experience with them, is a boat all about business the majority of the time. These guys have worked their way into the top shell on the team and are doing all they can to make the boat as fast and efficient as possible. They also are trying to protect their seats from any competitors in the 2v. As the most competitive event in most regattas, it makes sense for these guys to have the most competitive attitudes. What is different about the 1v is how they interact with each other. What I see are guys that are doing whatever it takes to make their boat faster and they communicate mostly for that reason. Of course, there is a lot of support for each other and they do enjoy themselves, but their main focus is always on improving the shell and going faster, as it should be.

Chapter 11
Input

Advice. This is something every coxswain strives for from their coaches, rowers, and fellow coxswains, rarely do we actually manage to get it. For the most part, it is not their fault, with the rowers, the differences between rower and coxswain are many, which renders the two not similar in actually any way at all. Most coaches participated as rowers in the sport and therefore only know who is a good coxswain and who is not. Rarely can they give you details as to why you are or not a good coxswain and rarely still can they actually present input that will help you improve. When I said that this is a self taught position, I did not mean that it is for lack of trying on the coach's part or lack of suggestions on the rower's part. I just meant that the details of our job is not known to your rowers and sometimes not even your coaches. The other coxswains cannot be blamed either, as the competition among coxswains often turns into a blood battle for seats. Yes, rowers have this competition too, but there are eight seats they can compete for versus our one, and often there are more coxswains than boats. If you don't win, you sometimes don't race at all. So it is unlikely that other coxswains will be more than willing to give you some tips on how to beat them out of their boat. The result of all of this is that good advice is hard to come by, making this small section extremely valuable. Use it.

From my Coach

Coaching Expectations for Coxswains

The coxswain must maintain the following set of priorities at all times: First, the coxswain must always ensure the safety of each of their rowers. Second, the coxswain must ensure the best competitive advantage of their crew. Third, the coxswain must ensure the safety of the shell itself. Lastly, the coxswain should help the coach, be mindful of water and wind conditions, and encourage and motivate their crew.

The first priority is the biggest. As the person steering the shell, the coxswain must not only attempt to avoid hitting things, but be aware of other shells on the water, the motorboats surrounding them and the conditions they are rowing in to be sure that each rower within the boat is safe from harm. The coxswain must always be willing to make the necessary calls and moves to ensure safety.

The next most important priority is far less important than the first, but remains a key part of the coxswain's job, the competitive advantage. The coxswain should do all that is necessary to ensure that their crew has the most fair and advantageous circumstances for success. The coxswain

87

should never allow another crew to intimidate or interfere with the racing of their crew, even if it means risking the integrity of the shell, but not the safety of the rowers. The coxswain should always be prepared to force other crews to relent to their needs and demands when the competitive advantage is at risk. This also means the coxswain should have their shells even with their competition and aligned for the race well before the coach or race officials make the calls to start the race. A coxswain should never be adjusting the physical positioning of the shell as the race officials start the race.

Next, the coxswain must be responsible for protecting the shell itself. They are the first person in charge of protecting the shell when they are in the coxswain seat. This holds true even over the coach. The only time a coxswain has the right or permission to override the coach's or official's commands are when the shell itself or the safety of the rowers therein is risked. The coxswain may make a calculated risk to the shell itself should the competitive advantage be risked, however.

Lastly, the coxswain must understand the needs of its crews daily and respond adequately. The coxswain is not a caretaker or protector of the crew's mental state, but should work with the crew to extract the most from them. They should be ready and willing to demand the most of their crews daily. On the water, the coxswain is not a friend to any in the boat, but an authority that must demand and command respect for and from the crew.

In short, a coxswain should be quick minded, decisive and clear headed at all times, ready to make necessary calls and expertly aware of the immediate needs of their crew, all while be willing and comfortable with being "the bad guy."

The coxswain should understand that screaming is not always the best means to motivate a crew. Coxswains should take time and effort to learn who their rowers are, why they want to win and what they expect from themselves and their crewmates in order to be effective in motivating them on the race course. The coxswain should always feel completely aware of their surroundings and in control at all times and should convey that confidence to their crews through their interactions with them daily.

From rower Drew Poloski

If I were to look for the best coxswain ever, some of the first things I would look for would be perfectionism, aggression, and not to mention the ability to steer a boat. This "best" coxswain can make the boat go faster by inspiring the rowers in their boat to pull harder, fix their technical problems, thus making the boat faster. Skipping numbers is my biggest pet peeve, so a coxswain that also has OCD is never a bad thing. While it may be a physical race for the rowers, it is a mental race for the coxswains, and this "perfect cox" would be aggressive before, during, and after races and practices. This coxswain would also have to take every practice and race seriously. During practice a coxswain may not be physically doing anything, but they can help rowers to improve their technical flaws, and I always like knowing what I need to fix and how to fix it. A good coxswain knows all of the rowers' mentalities on and off the water and knows how to motivate all of the rower's in their boat. I know from personal experiences that coxswains usually know their rowers limits better than their rowers do, and can push them to their maximum potential. So whether you love each other or hate each other, rower's need coxswains and coxswains need rowers regardless, so let's all try to get along.

From Rower AJ DeSantis
Who Was Previously A Coxswain

As a rower who was said communist coxswain mentioned previously, I prefer a coxswain who is focused and strategic over one that is encouraging. No amount of encouragement can make up for a powerful race strategy. If you are new to coxing I suggest that you are always aware of your surroundings. In a race this is important so you are able to make proper calls. Also, even if you don't know what you are doing, always make it look like you do. If your crew isn't confident in your abilities then that is just one more thing that will distract them from doing their jobs.

From rower Connor Watson

Successful rowers are, by and large, rather peculiar people. Whether out of sentiment, egotism, or sheer doggedness a varsity rower has endured. Rowing is a miserable excuse for a hobby or sport and more closely resembles military training or the cultivation of rice in water-logged paddys-- hard-work, day in day out, indefinitely. The dark core of the sport is that a boat that is level in the water and strong will always be very fast. So long as more power gets into the water in your boat than in the competitions', and if your boat remains perfectly flat throughout, you will win the race.

This is where the coxswain comes into play. In a rower's novice year coxswains first appear to keep the boats on course (another form of level), then proceed to critique the rowers form, and finally begin to supplement, substitute for the rower's own will during pieces. The coxswain beings to function as reservoir of important information, important information on getting power into water and keeping boats flat. They get steadily more confident and--with luck-- learn how to steer straight. They point out mistakes more and more often, and the health of their egos become tied to boat speed. The rower has a series of confused feelings about his coxswain at this point. The coxswain is helping the boat go fast, fast boats win, and rowers love to win only slightly less than they love to breathe. On the other hand its rather presumptuous to get snappy with someone who is trying to cough up their own lungs in a futile attempt to get air after a race; especially if you have never rowed lost a race yourself.

Very few rowers can understand coxswains, and many coxswains cannot really understand the mentality of high level rowers. Both have hunted their goals --rowing and coxing respectively--with the kind of single mindedness that makes a contrary perspective nonsensical when it is heard. The coxswain has the best overall view of boat speed, rush, timing, wind conditions, the competitions position and skill, course condition, bow dip, roll-up. But the rowers are the ones who go out and bleed for it.

From rower Hunter Kempf

The thing I look for in a coxswain is not someone who is intense and always screaming to the point that you can't understand them. As a rower I prefer the calm levelheaded approach of a coxswain granted some form of anger and aggressiveness is always good. When a coxswain goes into the race prepared for every situation and can call a command at the right time and can keep the crew motivated that is the best type of coxswain. When a crew is going down the course, especially in a five-kilometer race, you need a coxswain who knows what to say and how to say it to get the crew to do it properly and well. Great coxswains are rare things that don't come around often and when you get one in your boat that whole crew is lucky to get the expertise and strength that comes with them. Most people believe that coxswains only have a use on water, but that is anything but true. Coxswains are actually incredibly helpful when Erg testing as they can motivate you and make you finish the test with strength and power. It's also easy to forget about coxswains when in practice and do your own thing, some advice for rowers if you are possibly reading this book. Don't ever forget about the coxswain always pay attention and to the coxswain reading this book always make sure your rowers are focused and pay attention to you. Make sure that these rowers actually have something to hear like critique though the long periods of silence that make the rowers uncomfortable and irritable or they will lose focus and always be saying something negative about the shell, or about each other, or just in general. Another note is to try not to be too repetitive. Do not say the same thing over and over again, for example, I know I don't want to hear "drive!" nine times in a row during a piece. If you are learning to be a coxswain and don't know much some simple advice that will save you aggravation from the rowers is to stay on task and always focus on practice or racing. As a rower, it is difficult to get along with a coxswain who doesn't know what they are doing and are always goofing off and not caring about the sport. To finish with, if you want to the rowers show respect to you and be friendly just show them that you can work hard and care about them and the sport.

From coxswain Chloe Sink, 3 year captain of the men's team

There is no phenomenal advice on how to succeed as a coxswain because ultimately it will be your job to determine in what way you will find excellence.
I was not an outstanding coxswain, I lost a lot. But I also learned a hell of a ton more from my losses than from my

victories. You'll lose as well; this is one of the few certainties I can offer you, but my hope is that you will gain something from every single one of these failures. On the basis of my horrible writing ability I will offer you the advice that I would hope someone would give to me:

1. <u>Your mistakes only define you if you permit them to</u>. If you allow your shortcomings to constantly plague you attention then you will see your performance degrade to the point that all of your horrors will become the reality.

2. <u>"Fake it til' you make it"</u> is a common phrase passed among coxswains mostly because we are expected to know everything at every moment. Which is something that by human nature is impossible and if you are capable of this I have some serious questions regarding how you spend your free time. So for all of us normal people we've got to bullshit it a bit. "Of course I know where we're going" "yeah, they're making a move" "This is what coach wants" were some phrases I commonly threw out though I had absolutely no idea what was going on. As long as your crew felt comfortable so do you.

Standards

3. <u>Know your rowers:</u> what makes them tick, why they put themselves through this hell, what they do in their free time, what are their goals, what makes them laugh, who makes them laugh, what makes them nervous, how can you fix it?

4. <u>Don't back off:</u> you are competing for a seat just like the rowers and I can promise you that coxswains are just as cut throat, if not more. (I was never good at this and I would highly encourage that you at least offer a little bit of pressure on your competitors)

5. <u>Love the sport:</u> I know this seems a little bit ridiculous to say but you really need to. Your seat is all about passion, infusing a desire to win into your crew so you damn well better want it. My advice you be to learn about rowing, the more details you add the clearer and more impressive this art form will become.

6. <u>Respect:</u> Earn it.

7. <u>Humility:</u> Is the greatest character trait any athlete can possess and a coxswain is no exception. Every victory should be accredited to the crew and the coach. Every success falls onto hard work and not right. You deserve nothing and earn everything.

Please remember that :

"Success is the child of drudgery and perseverance. It cannot be coaxed or bribed; pay the and it is yours" -Orison Marden

In conclusion

You will generally not be able to get people to talk so openly about what they want in a coxswain and what they prefer. It is just something that is avoided in common conversation on the team. There are so few coxswains and we are such strong characters that the level of tension and competition between us is evident. The more you advance as a coxswain and the more serious you become about your job, the less people will be inclined to tell you what they want, and the more they will expect you to just know. In reference to my chapter on motivation, everyone is motivated differently and has different details in their expectations of a coxswain.

 So take this advice to heart and know that it is just from a small group of people and will definitely not represent the entirety of rowers.

From College Coxswain Daniel Vital

Trust and Respect

Trust is the most important quality for a coxswain. A great coxswain has the most loyal rowers. Rowers should never look outside of the boat because they trust their coxswain knows the best path. It is important to earn the trust of your rowers. Easy ways to do this

- Workout with the rowers. You are part of the team as well.

- Learn how to row if possible. Erging with the rowers help them see that you understand the pain they go through.

- Lead runs if possible and encourage those who are struggling in any workout. Do not be condescending be genuine and honest.

- Own up to every mistake you make. Try not to take insults too personally.

- **No matter how nervous you are, never show it!**

Loryn Schopke

Chapter 12
Failures

Ok so it sucks to make mistakes when you think you're the only one who has ever messed up. Usually people are willing to bring up their own embarrassing past as a way to make you feel better. Coxswains don't do that. It takes a long time for people to forget our mistakes so we tend to make sure they are never brought up unnecessarily. Well here are some failures that I have both witnessed and experienced. You are not alone.

I thought I would never race again

During a race last year at a hex meet (meaning that there were 6 teams) I was racing in the 2v towards the middle/end of the day. It was hugely windy and it was located at one of the participating team's boathouses. Said team tends not to set up the race course very well and not really orchestrate it well. Anyway, before the race, one of the coaches for the women's' team launches my boat and gets all up in my boat's business wanting to know every detail of our race plan (which wasn't all that detailed), and leaves me with some input. This is what she says to me; "Ok so you've been doing really really well and everyone is watching you so you better do well, you got this."

Needless to say I ended up not having it.

As I said before, the team hosting into the regatta tends not to set up the course all that well. When the boats in my race get aligned, I end up being pointed at the milk jug they use as a lane marker. Good start. So, the race gets going and I get past the milk jug and everything is fine. Literal plot twist, the course has developed a curve due to the wind. EVERY COXSWAIN KNOWS THIS EXCEPT ME APPARENTLY. So, the fun begins and I slowly move into the lane next to mine (only because my line is straight and the course is not), and I get yelled at by an official. This is where I screw up. I take a sharp turn to get back in my lane, which slows down my boat tremendously. After that point, nothing really goes right for me in general. One of my rowers takes it upon himself to convince my stroke seat to approach my coach and tell him that it was a boat decision to remove me from the shell AFTER ONE MISTAKE, and it actually works. I was removed from that boat for the remainder of the season, but not before this next failure.

How said communist got his name

Some time has passed after that wonderful incident, and the guys are seat racing again, myself included. Now, I was following this other coxswain's point as his boat was ahead of mine. The guys had just finished one of the pieces not 20 seconds prior when I run head on into a shell going in the opposite direction. Now this shell was going against traffic entirely and ended up directly in my blind spot. Of course, it was my fault for not checking my blind spot, and I will share in the responsibility for that incident 50/50 with him. I'm just saying though, who goes against traffic???

The first of many

Before any of that happened, I started the first of many breakages at our boathouse in the fall of last year. Technically we had broken a lot of skegs and steering but this was the first shell breakage that we could actually pinpoint fault for. What happened was, in the fall of last year, practice was over for the day and we were all heading in to the dock. It was pitch black which makes trying to dock way more difficult than it usually is. Long story short, I come in at a really bad angle, really fast and I wedge the bow of the shell under the dock and get it stuck. When we finally got it free, the damage to the shell included a small hole in the bow, a lost bow ball, and a bunch of scratched off paint. It was fairly embarrassing and degrading and I think I cried for an hour that evening. Rough stuff.

The second of many

This story will be short. Basically, a friend of mine did the exact same thing I did except she tore the entire bow off the shell. She now has it on display in her room as it was a gift from our coach. ("She" is Chloe by the way I'm just saying).

Google

I highly suggest looking up coxing failure videos. Not only are they hilarious, but they can make you feel better about your own mess ups. I suggest the St. Ignatius crash video, this chick steers directly into a pole, it's great.

Like I said, you will make mistakes so I suggest you embrace them, own up to them, and learn from them. If you make a mistake, lay low for a bit and build yourself back up. Just do your best every day and it will pay off.

Chapter 13
Final Thoughts
Notes

Of course, I am not a professional and therefore I am not going to know everything and be correct about everything I say. This has all worked for me, so this is what I know. I know when I first started coxing I scrounged the internet looking for a coxswain guide that didn't cost $90 and wasn't an internet PDF file. So I hope you found this helpful in some way, and I wish you luck in your coxing endeavors. The most I can ever really say is to find your own coxing style, know your crew, love the sport, and love your team. They can give you so much more than you could ever expect to receive from a group of people. This sport has taught me so much about myself and given me the best friends and memories that I could ask for. I just hope that when all is said and done for you, that you can take away just as much as I have from being a part of this sport called crew. I have included some blank pages for any notes you wish to take or things you need to remind yourself of. Good luck.

Standards

Notes

Loryn Schopke

Standards

Loryn Schopke

Standards

Loryn Schopke

Standards

Loryn Schopke

Standards

Loryn Schopke

Made in the USA
San Bernardino, CA
13 November 2018